255017

PROJECT

D0235944

Guess what I am

illustrated by Anni Axworthy

WALKER BOOKS
AND SUBSIDIARIES
LONDON · BOSTON · SYDNEY

What am I?

I'm a kind of cat,
like this kitten.

This is
my stripy
fur.

in the jungle.

Tigers are the biggest cats in the world.

What am I?

I'm a kind of fish,
but I don't live in a bowl.

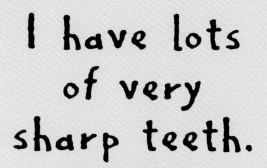

I have lots
of very
sharp teeth.

e a big
fin on
back.

as long as two cars.

A Great white
shark has two rows of teeth
at the top and two at the bottom.

What am I?

I like to gnaw on things,
just like these mice do.

is is my wide flat tail.

rivers.

I'm

bea

Beavers make their dams out of logs and twigs.

What am I?

I have wings like this parrot, but I can't fly.

This is my
favourite food.

This is
my beak.

I live near the icy South Pole.

There are 18 different sorts of penguin. I'm a King penguin.

What am I?

This puppy is a kind of dog,
and so am I.

is
my
ears.

This is my
bushy tail.

in a den underground.

I'm glad
I don't live
in a den.

I'm a fo

Foxes make their dens
in towns as well as in
the countryside.

All our names have got muddled up. Can you help us to sort them out?

Beaver

Penguin

FALKIRK COUNCIL
LIBRARY SUPPORT
FOR SCHOOLS

Tiger

Fox

Shark

First published 1998 by Walker Books Ltd
87 Vauxhall Walk, London SE11 5HJ

2   4   6   8   10   9   7   5   3

Series concept and design by Louise Jackson

Words by Louise Jackson and Paul Harrison

Wildlife consultant: Martin Jenkins

Text © 1998 Walker Books Ltd
Illustrations © 1998 Anni Axworthy

This book has been typeset in Joe Overweight.

Printed in Singapore

British Library Cataloguing in Publication Data
A catalogue record for this book is available
from the British Library.

ISBN 0-7445-6213-9